Copyright © 2025 Jennifer Jones
All copyright laws and rights reserved.
Published in the U.S.A.
For more information, email info@ninjalifehacks.tv
Paperback ISBN: 978-1-63731-969-7
Hardcover ISBN: 978-1-63731-971-0
eBook ISBN: 978-1-63731-970-3

Find the Gingerbread on Strike lesson plans at ninjalifehacks.tv

They'd lost their legs and candy arms.
Their gumdrops popped off clean.
"Stop biting off our heads!" they cried.
"This baking thing's obscene!"

The gingerbread peeked through the door,
then smiled, proud and wide.
They saw the fun, the gentle touch,
and marched right back inside.

There were games and songs and cookie talks,
and not one bite all day.
The gingerbread felt safe again
and chose to stay and play.

Now every year they bake with care
and treat each cookie with pride.
They decorate, admire, and laugh,
but never eat all the sides!

Design Your Gingerbread Pal!

Give them a name, style, and holiday wish!

Cookie name: _____
Favorite outfit: _____
What they wish for: _____
_____
_____
_____

Draw your Gingerbread Pal here!

www.ingramcontent.com/pod-product-compliance
Lightning Source LLC
Chambersburg PA
CBHW041713160426
43209CB00018B/1826